CW00539129

04094

The Magic Mouse
Dictionary
of Computers
and Information Technology

by
Chris Ward-Johnson,
William Gould
and the Magic Mouse

Illustrations and layout by
Laughing Gravy Design

CHERRYTREE BOOKS

A Cherrytree Book

Designed and produced by A S Publishing
Illustrations and layout by Gary Dillon & Phil Jolly at
Laughing Gravy Design

First published 2001
by Cherrytree Press
327 High Street
Slough
Berkshire
SL1 1TX

Copyright © Evans Brothers Limited 2001

British Library Cataloguing in Publication Data
Ward-Johnson, Chris
Magic Mouse Dictionary of Computers and Information Technology
1. Information technology
2. Computers
I. Title
II. Gould, William
III. Dictionary of Computers and Information Technology
004'.03
ISBN 1 84234 056 5

Printed in Dubai by Oriental Press

Contents

Dip in where you like or look on pages 4-7 to find the word you want

The number after each word is the page where you will find its meaning.

Your computer

A personal computer (PC) can do lots of useful things. You can use it to write letters and e-mails. You can do homework on it. You can play music and watch movies on it. You can draw pictures and play games on it. And lots more.

Active When you double-click on an icon to open a window or click on a window that is already open, it becomes active and ready to use.

Application Program or set of programs that performs a specific task.

Backup Copy of documents or programs. Always play safe and back up your work. Then it will not be a disaster if you accidentally erase something you need.

Bit Short for binary digit. Computers treat information as a collection of 0s and 1s, binary digits. Electricity flowing equals 1, not flowing equals 0.

Booting Starting up a computer.

Byte A set of eight bits.

CD Short for compact disk. This kind of disk can store a lot of information in a tiny space. CDs can store music, pictures or computer files.

CD-ROM CD that you cannot erase. CD-ROMs hold computer programs and large encyclopedias.

Remember to back up your work!

Central processing unit *see* CPU.

Chip *see* Microchip.

Clicking Pressing and quickly releasing a mouse button. To double-click, press and release the button twice. You will soon know when to click once and when to double-click.

Command A word such as Print or Run that the computer recognizes as an instruction to do something.

Compact disk *see* CD.

Components Parts that make up a computer, including the CPU, disk drives, monitor and keyboard.

CPU Short for central processing unit, the microchip that is the brain of the computer, making it work and run programs.

Cursor Line, arrow or other shape that shows you where you are on screen. You can move it about using the keyboard or mouse.

Data Facts and figures fed into a computer to be stored and examined by it.

Data processing Handling, storing and organizing data to produce useful information.

Desktop Screen that appears soon after you switch on your computer. It shows icons that you can move about with a mouse, like papers on a real desk.

Desktop computer Computer that can sit on your desk.

DVD

CD-ROM

Dialog box

Dialog box Onscreen panel that asks you to take actions, make choices or change settings.

Digital Representing information, including text, music and pictures, by numbers. Digital clocks show the time in figures. Digital computers reduce all information to a string of 0s and 1s, or bits.

Digital versatile disk *see* DVD.

Disk *see* CD; CD-Rom; Floppy disk; Hard disk. Disk may also be spelled disc.

Disk drive Part of a computer in which a CD, CD-ROM, floppy disk or hard disk is inserted or housed. The computer spins the disk in the drive and either reads

data from it or writes information on it for storage.

Diskette A floppy disk.

Double-click *see* Clicking.

DVD Short for digital versatile disk. This stores far more data than a CD or CD-ROM. It easily holds a full-length movie.

File Collection of data, such as a word-processed document or a program, stored in a computer's memory or on a disk.

Floppy disk Small disk, or diskette, which can store only a small amount of information.

Floppy disk

Folder Place on a computer where you can store related files.

Format To run a special program on a disk that makes it ready to hold computer files. Any data already on it will be erased.

Gigabyte About 1 billion bytes. Strictly speaking, it equals 1,024 x 1,024 x 1,024 = 1,073,741,824 bytes.

Hard disk Disk inside the hard drive that holds the computer's operating system. It starts spinning when the computer is booted. You can store programs and files on it.

Hardware The computer and all its components and peripherals.

Help Part of a program that explains how to use the program.

Icon Picture that represents a file or program on the desktop.

Install To set up a program on your computer by copying all its files to your hard disk.

Instruction Line in a program that tells a computer what to do.

Interface Device or program through which you use a computer.

Keyboard Form of typewriter on which you can type words and numbers into a computer. It also has keys for special functions.

Kilobyte About 1,000 bytes. Strictly speaking, 1,024 bytes.

Laptop computer Portable computer small enough to rest on your lap.

Laser Device that produces an intense, narrow beam of light. It is used to read data from, or write data to, CDs or DVDs.

Leads *see* Power cords.

Load To place data or a program into a computer's memory.

Megabyte About 1,000,000 bytes. Strictly speaking, 1,048,567 bytes.

Megahertz One million hertz, a measure of a computer's speed.

Memory Set of microchips in a computer that hold data. *See* RAM; ROM.

Menu List of choices or actions.

Microchip Tiny piece of silicon with thousands of electronic circuits on it that enable a computer to work. Also called a chip.

Help tells you what to do if you don't know

Microprocessor A computer's CPU. Microprocessors also power radios, video recorders, and so on.

Monitor Screen linked to a computer. It is sometimes called a visual display unit (VDU).

Mouse Device plugged into a computer that enables you to control an onscreen pointer. It has one to three buttons. It lets you point at and select an item, drag it about, open windows or start programs. *See* Clicking.

Multitasking Running several programs at once.

Notebook computer Computer small enough to fit in a briefcase.

OK Option in a dialog box. If you click on it or press the Enter or Return key, the program carries out the action you have chosen.

Operating system Set of programs loaded after your computer is turned on. They control the way it runs and communicates with you.

Peripheral External device linked to a computer. Peripherals include printers and scanners.

Personal computer Computer designed for use in homes, schools and offices. Also called a PC.

Platform Type or brand of computer or operating system you use.

Pointer *see* Cursor; Mouse.

Port Socket on computer used for plugging in peripherals.

Power cords Cables, or leads, that connect a computer and its peripherals to the power supply.

Power supply Electricity supplied from the mains or a battery.

Program List of instructions written in computer language for a computer to carry out.

Programmer Someone who writes computer programs.

Programming language Any of several computer languages used for writing programs. They include BASIC and C++.

Keep your computer and mouse clean.

RAM Short for random-access memory. RAM is used by the computer to store data while a program is running. You can change the data as much as you want, but if you want to keep it, you must save it to your hard disk before you end the program or turn off the computer.

ROM Short for read-only memory. This memory stores data permanently. Usually you cannot change it.

Run To set a program working, usually by double-clicking an icon or typing in a command.

Save To store on disk the data from a program. *See* Load.

Silicon Common substance found in the earth's crust and used for making microchips.

Software General name for computer programs.

Store Anything that can hold data from the CPU. RAM is a temporary store. A disk is more permanent.

Upgrade New version of a program or piece of hardware.

Window Rectangular area on screen in which you can see icons and work on documents.

DANGER! ELECTRICITY

NEVER stick your fingers or any other object into a wall socket.
NEVER stick your fingers or metal objects into a disk drive.
NEVER jolt or shake your computer, especially if it is on.
NEVER take the back off your computer. If you need help, ask an adult.
KEEP liquids well away from your computer.
TURN OFF your computer before you plug a keyboard, monitor, mouse or printer into it.

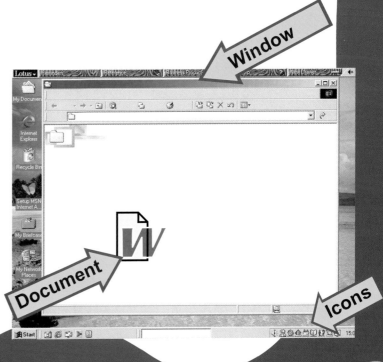

Window

Document

Icons

Words, words, words

A computer cannot make you a good writer, but it can help you make your work and your letters look good. Do not worry if you cannot type well. You can change what you write as much as you like. When you are happy with your work, save it and print as many copies as you like.

ASCII code Each letter, each number and each punctuation mark has a code called an ASCII code. When you press a key, the computer knows which letter to display or print by matching the key you pressed to the right code. ASCII means American Standard Code for Information Interchange.

Cut and paste Way of selecting and moving text in a document. In most word processors, you drag your mouse over text to highlight it. Then, by pressing certain keys or making certain choices on an Edit menu, you can cut text out of a document and paste it back somewhere else in the same document or in a different one.

Delete or **Erase** Using certain keys and other means, you can remove text or pictures from documents, or files from a disk.

Desktop publishing Special software programs that enable you to mix text and pictures to produce professional-looking documents, such as a pamphlet, brochure, magazine or book.

Document Pages on which you can write or draw onscreen and which you can print out.

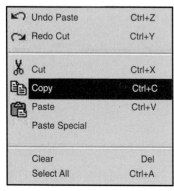

	Undo Paste	Ctrl+Z
	Redo Cut	Ctrl+Y
	Cut	Ctrl+X
	Copy	**Ctrl+C**
	Paste	Ctrl+V
	Paste Special	
	Clear	Del
	Select All	Ctrl+A

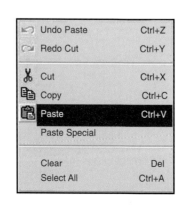

	Undo Paste	Ctrl+Z
	Redo Cut	Ctrl+Y
	Cut	Ctrl+X
	Copy	Ctrl+C
	Paste	**Ctrl+V**
	Paste Special	
	Clear	Del
	Select All	Ctrl+A

PASTE

Edit When you edit a document, you correct mistakes in it, shorten it, or make other changes to it.

Erase *see* Delete.

Font Particular design, or shape, and size of typeface used for the letters and numbers in a document. This text is in a face called Arial, its size is 14pt, and its style is Roman (upright). So its font is 14pt Arial Roman.

Frame In desktop publishing, an onscreen box that holds a piece of text or a picture. You can move it around using a mouse or cut and paste it.

Hard copy Document that is printed on paper. Hard copy output by a computer is called a printout.

Hard copy

Inkjet printer Printer that fires fine jets of quick-drying ink through tiny nozzles in a printer cartridge onto paper.

Insert You can put a picture, a table or some other item into a document, usually by making a choice from an Insert menu.

The rat sat on the mat!

Read your work. Spell checkers cannot read thoughts.

Laser printer Printer that uses tiny pinpoint lasers to trace the image of a page onto a light-sensitive drum. Dry ink called toner transfers the image to paper to print the page.

Macro Set of commands or actions grouped to form a single command. You create a macro by recording all the actions first. Then you run it with a mouse click or by pressing certain keys. Macros save time.

Merge To combine two or more files to make one. In word processing, you can place one document at a specific point within another. *See also* Mail merge.

OCR Short for optical character recognition. A program that enables a computer to recognize the shapes of type printed on paper and then turn these patterns into electronic text for word processing. Most scanners come with OCR software.

Page One side of a sheet of paper. Breaking a document into pages in a word processor is called pagination. A page is also a screenful of data.

Paste *see* Cut and paste.

Print cartridge Container filled with ink, or toner, for use by a printer.

Printer Any of several types of machine that outputs a computer's work as hard copy. Most modern printers are laser printers or inkjets.

Printout *see* Hard copy.

Ruler Onscreen scale that allows you to set line length, page width and tab positions in a word-processed document.

Scroll To move through the text of a document on-screen using a mouse. You can scroll up and

Toolbar

down or left and right.

Spell checker Tool in word processing program that checks the words in a document against an electronic dictionary. It will pick up many errors but will not notice if you have missed a word or used the wrong word.

Stationery Writing paper, printer paper, print cartridges, labels and similar items used in an office.

Tab Key that lets you jump to a set point in a line of type. You use it to indent paragraphs and line up text and figures in columns.

Table Information set out in rows and columns.

Text Information in words rather than pictures.

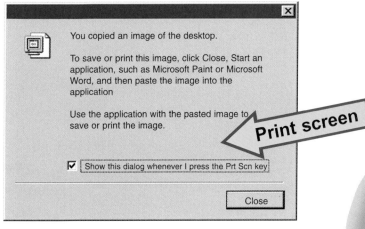

You copied an image of the desktop.

To save or print this image, click Close, Start an application, such as Microsoft Paint or Microsoft Word, and then paste the image into the application

Use the application with the pasted image to save or print the image.

☑ Show this dialog whenever I press the Prt Scn key

Close

Print screen

Toolbar Row of icons, or 'buttons', usually along the top of a screen. Click on them to carry out tasks such as opening documents, making tables and printing.

Word processor Purpose-built computer or computer program that you use to type, edit, store and print text documents.

Wrap To carry a line of text over to the next line. You can wrap text round a picture like this. In word-wrapping, only whole words are carried over.

small TYPE

BIG

TYPE

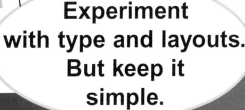

Experiment with type and layouts. But keep it simple.

Keeping track

Can you remember who scored the winning goal in last year's football final or who won in 1955? Of course you cannot. But if you tell it to, your computer will keep all sorts of records for you. Organize your data in a database, and you will always be able to find, or retrieve, information when you need it.

Access Action or process of using a database or retrieving information from it.

Accounts package Set of programs that allows you to record your income and what you spend. It will add figures and do many other calculations, and lay them out in columns on a spreadsheet.

Address *see* pages 44 and 53.

Address book Program that lists the names and addresses of people in alphabetical order. An address book is a simple database.

Calculator Device that can add, subtract, multiply and divide numbers, and do really difficult sums for you. Personal computers usually come with calculator programs.

Cell Spreadsheet programs and tables use a screen divided into rows and columns that form a grid. Each box in the grid is a cell. Each cell has a cell name, such as A3 or B5, to help you keep track of where you are.

Chart Drawing that shows data in picture form, for example as a graph. Many database and spreadsheet programs are able to convert data automatically and draw it on screen ready for printing.

Column Group of items in a table, or cells in a spreadsheet, laid out vertically from top to bottom.

Database Organized collection of data held in a computer, consisting of a series of records. The data in the records can be arranged or looked at in various ways. Address books, stock lists and dictionaries are all types of database.

Field All the records in a database are split into fields, or separate classes of information.

An address, for example, may have various fields: first name, last name, house number, street, town, and postcode. Your database can organize the information so that you can get a list of all the people who live in Swindon, or all the people called Mouse.

File An entire collection of records making up a database.

Find Menu option that searches for a particular word or other item in a document. In the main menu Find helps you search for lost documents.

Forecast A guess about what will happen in the future if certain things turn out to be true. Spreadsheet programs can predict what will happen if, for example, you change one or two numbers.

Information retrieval Finding and recovering specific information from databases.

Keep your files in order.

Information technology (IT)
The study or business of using computers and telecommunications equipment for storing, obtaining or sending information.

Mail merge Part of a program that allows you to combine a document with a database of addresses. By mail-merging a letter with an address book, you type the document only once but address copies of it personally to each person in your address book.

Maths program Software that enables you to do calculations and check your solutions.

Merge To combine database files. The word is also short for mail merge.

Record Complete collection of data within a database file. A record is like a single entry in an address book. Records are divided into fields. *See also* Field.

Relational database Database formed from the joining of two or more linked databases. It lets you recover information in more ways than a simple database can.

Row Group of items in a table or of cells in a spreadsheet that go across, rather than down.

Search To look for specific data in a database. Computers can search faster in databases that have been sorted into order.

Searchkey Word or name that stands for an item to be found in

Spreadsheet

a database. When you search, be as specific as possible. If you type in the name Smith only, you may not find the person you are looking for straight away. If you type in Peter Smith, you will have more chance.

Spreadsheet Type of program used by accountants. Columns and rows of figures typed into a grid can be added up, multiplied, and so on. Spreadsheets are also useful for other types of lists and tables.

Work out roughly what your totals should be in case you press the wrong key.

In the picture

With the right program you can turn your computer into a paintbox. You can work on pictures the program gives you or draw or paint your own pictures with a mouse or light pen. You can scan in photographs, touch them up and print them. You can store photos on CD and view them as slide shows. You can even make your own movies.

Animation Way of building up a set of images and then showing them in quick succession so that they appear like a moving picture.
Aspect ratio Relationship between the width of a picture and its height. When you change the size of a picture, you can stop it from becoming distorted by preserving the aspect ratio.

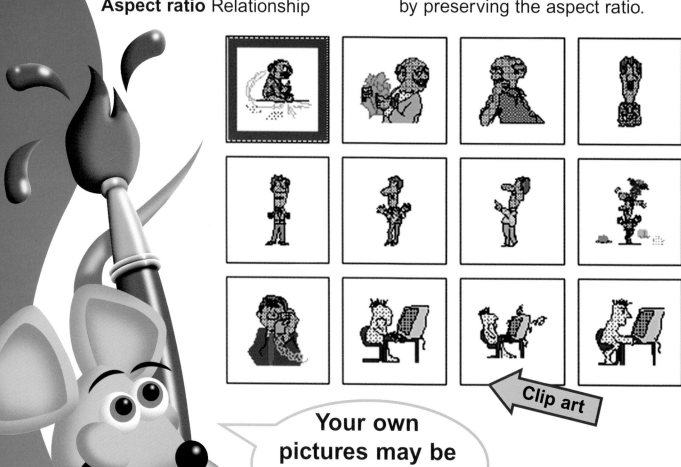

Clip art

Your own pictures may be better than clip art.

Bitmap

Any change in height will automatically be matched by a change in width.

Bitmap A picture or image is made up of tiny dots called pixels. A bitmap is a file in which the computer stores information about each pixel's colour, position and so on, coded as a series of bits (0s and 1s). GIF and JPEG files are bitmaps.

CAD Short for computer-aided design. CAD programs allow architects and engineers to make technical drawings using three-dimensional (3D) effects to show various views of solid objects.

Clip art Simple pre-drawn pictures that you can add to a document. Paint programs and desktop publishing software often include clip art. You can also download it from the internet.

Digital camera Camera that uses no film but takes photographs electronically. A lens focuses the image onto a light-sensitive component called a charge-coupled device (CCD). This turns

Digital camera

the image into a pattern of 0s and 1s that can be fed into a computer.

Display The image displayed on a computer screen is composed of dots called pixels (short for picture elements). These are red, green, or blue. Mixed together, they appear to form all the other colours. The size and number of pixels counted across and down the screen determines the resolution of the display or of an image. The more pixels, the smoother the display. *See* High-resolution; Low-resolution; Image.

GIF Short for graphics interchange file. Type of bitmap image file widely used on the world wide web. GIF files can be made quite small and so are quick to download or send by e-mail. It is also possible to produce animated GIFs. *See* Animation.

Graphics program Software that enables you to draw or edit pictures, design posters, prepare web pages and so on.

Graphics tablet Device shaped like a note-pad that lets you make free-hand drawings for display and storage by a computer. It senses the pressure of a pen and turns this pressure into electronic information.

High-resolution Display or image made up of a large number of

High Resolution

Low Resolution

24

pixels. In a high-resolution image, curves and sloping lines look smooth. A high-resolution screen display might be 1,024 pixels across by 768 pixels down. The resolution of a printed image is measured by the number of dots used for each horizontal inch (2.54 cm) of the image. High-resolution images are printed at 1,200 to 2,400 dots per inch (dpi).

Image Picture, especially one formed in a camera by the focusing of a lens or produced on a computer screen or by a printer.

Image file Computer file that contains an image. It can be edited using a graphics or paint program. GIFs and JPEGs are types of image file. They condense the data needed to produce the image into small files.

JPEG Type of bitmap image file that is widely used on the world wide web. JPEGs usually take up more space than GIFs, but while a GIF is limited to 256 colours, a JPEG may have as many as 16 million. The name

stands for Joint Picture Experts Group.

Light pen Penlike device attached to a computer and used with certain screens. You can use a light pen to draw shapes directly on the screen and to change or move sections of the drawing.

Low-resolution A low-resolution screen display uses few colours and large pixels. In low-resolution images, curves and sloping lines appear jagged or stepped. A low-resolution display measures fewer than 640 pixels across by 480 pixels down and uses 256 colours or fewer. A low-resolution printed image is anything less than 300 dots per inch (dpi).

Rough your pictures on paper first.

25

Monochrome A monochrome image is one that is in black and white. A monochrome monitor or display uses only one colour along with black (which to a computer is really an absence of colour). Monochrome monitors may use white, green or orange.

MPEG A standard type of movie image file widely used on the world wide web. The name is short for Motion Picture Experts Group.

Multimedia A multimedia document, website or CD-ROM combines various information sources, including text, pictures, animation, sound, and movie or video clips.

Optical disk *see* Videodisk.

Paint program Graphics program that lets you use a variety of painting techniques.

Picture file *See* Image file.

Pixel *See* Bitmap; Display; High-resolution

Quicktime Standard form of movie image file widely used on the world wide web and in CD-ROM encyclopedias.

RGB Short for Red, Green, Blue, referring to the three separate video signals that build up a colour display.

Scanner Machine connected to a computer that makes a digital copy of a printed picture or a piece of text and passes it to the computer as an image or text file. Text files, produced using OCR, can be edited.

Sprite Shape that can be designed by someone using a computer and moved about the screen.

Video Movie content of a multimedia source of information. The word video is also short for videocassette recorder. In a television set or computer monitor, the video signal provides the picture being displayed.

Videodisk Early type of CD that could play sound and video material through a television. Also called an optical disk.

Scanner

Sounds great

With the right kind of equipment and software, you can use your computer to make sounds, show movies or videos, and play music. You can play CDs or compose music of your own.

Audio CD Compact disk (CD) that stores music and other sounds in electronic form. You play audio CDs on a CD player or in the CD drive of your computer.

CD-R (Recordable CD) Compact disk (CD) that you can record onto, but only once. Most up-to-date computers have CD-R drives that use lasers to record music tracks or computer files on CD-Rs. Many people record whole audio CDs or MP3 files on CD-Rs. Such activities may break the law on copyright.

CD-RW (Rewritable CD) Compact disk (CD) that you can record on, erase, and record on again.

Channel A path by which sound information is passed from one device to another, for example between a computer and a synthesizer. In a MIDI system, a computer can process information on up to 16 channels and so control 16 different instruments.

DVD see page 10.

Frequency We hear a sound because it makes the air vibrate near our ears. The number of vibrations in each second is the frequency of the sound and is measured in Hertz. The greater the frequency, the higher the pitch of the sound.

Long wavelength
low frequency

Short wavelength
high frequency

Hertz Basic unit of frequency, equalling one cycle per second. The unit takes its name from Heinrich Hertz (1857-1894), the German scientist who was the first person to transmit and receive radio waves.

Microphone Device used for recording sound as electrical signals. In a computer the sounds are in digital form. Computer microphones are used with internet phone or videoconferencing software, speech recognition programs, and for interactive programs such as foreign language courses.

MIDI Short for Musical Instrument Digital Interface. Electronic circuit that accepts and sends out sound information in digital form. MIDI circuits allow computers, musical instruments and synthesizers to work together. *See also* Channel.

Mixer

Recording music uses lots of memory.

Music keyboard

MIDI file Sequence of sounds or piece of music recorded on a computer using the MIDI programming language. It can be played back later.

Minidisk Pocket-sized disk similar to a floppy disk upon which you can record music more than once and listen to it on a minidisk player.

Mixer Computer program that lets you combine sounds from several channels when recording or playing music. Its screen display looks like a mixer desk in a commercial recording studio. You can use your mouse to control the volume of each channel by moving sliders on the screen. The program may be used with a sequencer.

Mono Sound recorded and played back or broadcast using only one channel is known as mono.

MP3 Way of recording and storing music digitally so that a computer user can listen to it over the internet or save it onto a PC. Some MP3 music files are of CD quality. You need a special machine called an MP3 player to

listen to them away from your computer.

MPEG Short for Motion Picture Experts Group. Way of storing and playing movies and video clips including sound on a computer. MPEG files often form part of a multimedia package such as a CD-ROM encyclopedia. They can be played while you are connected to the internet or saved onto your PC's hard disk and watched later.

Multimedia *see* page 26.

Music keyboard Electronic piano that enables you to compose and play music. Some keyboards have memory chips that can store the music you play and replay it later. Many keyboards can be plugged into a computer, allowing you to make use of the computer's sound card.

Panning Making sound move from one channel to another.

Patch One of many instrumental sounds, such as that of a piano or violin, that a synthesizer can produce. You can choose different patches using a program such as a sequencer.

29

Volume control

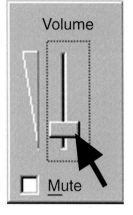

Playlist List of songs or CD tracks in a program that plays audio CDs or MIDI files. You can make your own lists and change the order as you like.

Real Audio Way of processing sound (either music or speech) so that it can be played over the internet. Radio programmes are broadcast over the internet in a continuous stream of Real Audio. Real Video allows TV broadcasts to be transmitted in the same way.

Record To store a sound, picture or movie on a computer. You can record sound and music from a cassette deck or CD player or by using a microphone. You can record a picture using a digital camera or scanner. Recording movies and videos needs complicated equipment and takes up a lot of computer memory and disk space.

Recordable CD *see* page 27.
Rewritable CD *see* page 27.
Sampling Converting music or sounds to a digital form that a computer can work with. Many pop songs use sampling. The musician takes a short sampled sound, such as a part of another piece of music, and changes it by computer, distorting it or repeating it over and over as part of his or her own song.

Sequencer Computer program that takes what you play on a music keyboard and turns it into a MIDI file. Many sequencer programs allow you to put in or edit the music using a mouse.

Sound card Extra circuits put into a computer to enable it to reproduce sounds

STEREO

through loudspeakers. A sound card contains a synthesizer. It may also have a socket called an input jack into which a microphone, music keyboard or other device can be plugged.

Sound file Any computer file containing recorded sound. MIDI files, Real Audio files and Wave files are types of sound file.

Stereo Short for stereophonic sound. Sound recorded and played back or broadcast using two or more channels. Hearing the sound from more than one direction makes it more realistic.

Synthesizer Set of special electronic circuits that can produce sounds and imitate different musical instruments.

Track On an audio CD, a track is a single song or piece of music. In a MIDI sequencer, a track is a single musical part or instrument or the channel used for it.

Wave file A way of storing a sound on a computer.

Use the mouse to control the volume.

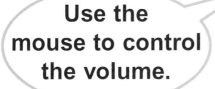

Game on

Although your computer is a serious piece of electronic equipment that can help with your work, it can also give you lots of fun - killing aliens, rescuing elves, or a game of football.

Action game Type of video game in which the player controls the action, either to move the plot along or just for the enjoyment of the game.

Adventure game Type of video game in which the player explores the world conjured up by the game and takes part in the story that unfolds. Adventure games include elements of action games, role-playing games and puzzle games. Classic adventure games include Myst and the Monkey Island series.

Arcade game Simple video game played on a purpose-built machine in an amusement arcade. Pong was the first arcade game.

Avatar In a chat room or an online role-playing game, an avatar is a graphical image that you choose to stand in for you. It can look like a person, animal or object.

Boss Opponent generated and controlled by the computer who is the fastest, cleverest and most villainous of all the opponents pitted against you in an action game.

Cartridge Removable unit that can be plugged into a computer

Boss

or games console and contains a program or games software. Often called a cart.

Cheat Code, group of keys or program that a player can use in a game to improve his playing skills or his character artificially.

Computer game or **PC game** Game to be played on a personal computer rather than on a console.

Console Purpose-built machine, controlled by microprocessors, on which players may run video games.

Dreamcast Games console made by the Japanese company Sega.

Driving game Type of computer game in which the player drives a vehicle in a race. Many of the games give the player a view from behind the driving wheel, others let the player see the whole car he or she is controlling.

Dungeons and Dragons One of the earliest and classic fantasy role-playing games. From 4 to 7 players, each with his or her own character, enter an imaginary world peopled by goblins, elves, monsters and so on. Originally a

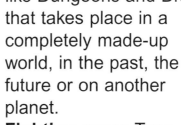

pen-and-paper game played around a table, it is now played over the internet.

Fantasy game Type of game, like Dungeons and Dragons, that takes place in a completely made-up world, in the past, the future or on another planet.

Fighting game Type of game in which the player has to beat a game-generated opponent in order to win. Most fighting games are played on consoles such as Playstation or Dreamcast. Most are too violent for children under 12 or 13.

First-person game Type of game in which the player sees the game world and everything that goes on in it through the 'eyes' of his character in the game.

Frag Another word for kill or destroy by shooting, used especially in online shooter games.

Game Boy Brand of hand-held games console made by Nintendo.

Gamer Person who plays video or computer games a lot.

Gaming The activity or hobby of playing video or computer games.

Hit point Unit measuring a character's strength, experience, and ability to defend himself or herself. In a role-playing game, a player's ability to stay in the game is measured in hit points. Hit points go up as a character becomes stronger or more skilful. If the character is wounded, he or she loses hit points. If the hit points fall to zero, the character is dead or knocked out.

Joystick Mechanical lever-like device that can be moved in various directions to control the position of an image or pointer on screen.

Lobby server Central computer on a network or on the internet that allows several players to gather together to start a new game, chat with each other and take part in any of several games going on at the same time. The lobby server keeps track of the players, allowing them to roam around looking for areas of interest.

Games console

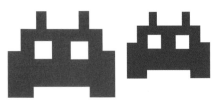

MMOG Short for massively multiplayer online game. Type of game played over the internet that allows thousands of players to take part.

MUD Short for Multi-user Dungeon. Type of role-playing internet game.

Nintendo Japanese company making games programs and consoles.

Online gaming Playing games over the internet.

PC game *see* Computer game

Piloting game Type of computer game in which the player flies an aircraft or spaceship. Piloting games include flight simulators for real aircraft.

Platform Type of action game in which the player's character has to leap to and from platforms.

Playstation Brand of games console manufactured by the Japanese company Sony.

Puzzle game Type of game in which the player wins by solving a puzzle.

Playing with friends can be more fun!

Real-time strategy (RTS) game
Type of fast-paced game in which the game program reacts immediately (that is, in real time) to the actions of the players. All the competitors perform their actions at the same time.

Role-playing game (RPG) Type of game that tells a story and involves several players, each one adopting the identity of a character within the game. The aim of the game is to complete a task (for example, to defeat a villain, rescue a princess or slay a monster). Role-playing games are often played on computers rather than consoles, and are popular among online gamers.

Sega Japanese company whose products include Sega Master System (SMS), Genesis (for which Sonic the Hedgehog was designed), Saturn, and Dreamcast.

Shooter Type of game in which the player's character shoots other characters. In a first-person shooter, the player sees the character being shot at through his own character's eyes.

Sport game Any of numerous games based on sports such as football, baseball, golf and so on.

Sony Japanese company that makes Playstation, audio and video equipment and games.

Strategy game Type of game in which players have to make decisions that take advantage of their opponent's weakness and ensure that they themselves are fully defended.

Third-person game Type of game that gives the player a complete view of the character he or she is controlling.

Turn-based game Type of game in which each player has a go while the others wait their turn.

Video game Game played on an electronic machine such as a console, computer or arcade machine, in which players use a control device to move points of light or images about on screen.

Virtual reality (VR) Illusion of reality produced by a computer. A landscape or fantasy world is created by feeding images, sounds and other sensations to users wearing special equipment. Virtual reality has serious applications, too, for example in surgery and in the remote handling of hazardous materials.

Zap Informal word for kill or frag.

Violence in real life hurts.

Owww!!!

Connecting to the world

If you hook your computer up to the telephone line you can share information with computers all over the planet. On the internet, you can talk to the world.

@ Stands for the word 'at'.

Access To gain entry to something. Accessing the internet means connecting your computer to it by modem and telephone. Accessing a network means opening a link with the network's server.

Access provider *see* ISP.

Acronym Initials used in place of whole words. See panel on page 40 for some examples.

ADSL Type of broadband internet connection.

Broadband Connection to the internet that can be more than ten times faster than telephone modem. ADSL and cable modems are types of broadband connection.

Cable modem Type of broadband internet connection.

Client Computer on a network or on the internet that can ask for and receive data from a central server.

co, com Short for company. It appears in e-mail and world wide web addresses to show that the owner of the address or site is a commercial company.

Country codes Each country has a special code used in domain names. *See* panel on page 41.

Cyberspace The world of the internet.

Dial-up service Service that links your computer to the internet over an ordinary telephone line. You access the internet only when you want to. Your computer's modem dials the telephone number of your ISP. The connection lasts only as long as the telephone line is open.

Domain name Part of an address that says what, and sometimes where, the owner of the address is. The domain name is the part of an e-mail address that comes after the @ sign. It consists of the name of a business, college or other organization, then an abbreviation, such as com or co (for companies) or edu or ac (for universities or colleges), and finally a country code, such as uk or nz. Many domain names ignore country codes.

Download When you use your computer to copy something from a server on the internet, you download it.

You can download e-mail, a page from the world wide web, or a program or document from an FTP server.

ACRONYMS

People on the internet use acronyms as a kind of shorthand to save time in e-mails. Here are some common ones.

AFAIK	As far as I know
AIR	As I recall
BTW	By the way
CU	See you
FYI	For your information
IMO	In my opinion
IYKWIM	If you know what I mean
LOL	Laughs out loud
MYOB	Mind your own business
OTT	Over the top
ROFL	Rolls on floor laughing
TIA	Thanks in advance
TTFN	Ta ta for now
TY	Thank you

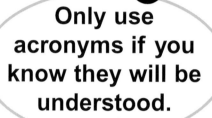

Only use acronyms if you know they will be understood.

File transfer protocol *see* FTP.

Firewall Software that protects a computer from being accessed by someone who does not have permission to do so. People with permission must use a user name and password to get through the firewall.

FTP (File transfer protocol) One of the methods for moving documents, programs and other data between computers connected to a network or the internet.

Hacker Person who tries to access files or programs on a computer without permission, either as a joke or to do harm.

Host Any computer connected to the internet.

Internet Worldwide network of computer networks linked by telephone, satellite or fibre-optic cable. It allows the movement of e-mail messages, the exchange of programs and other data, and includes the world wide web.

Internet safety There are some strange people on the internet.

Some adults pretend to be children, so be careful. See panel on page 43.

ISDN Short for integrated service digital network. Special kind of telephone connection that allows you to send and receive sound, pictures and all kinds of data in digital form very quickly and without loss of quality.

ISP (**Internet service provider**) Company paid to provide a link to the internet.

kbps Short for kilobits per second. This is the measure of the speed at which a modem transfers data.

Kilobit About 1,000 bits (actually 1,024 bits).

Leased line Permanent link to the internet over a special cable provided by an ISP for an annual fee. Leased lines are more expensive than dial-up services.

Log in or **Log on** Another term for access, especially when you have to use a password. Logging on to a website just means opening it in your browser.

Log out or **Log off** What you do when you end a session on a network or on the internet. You usually have to follow a certain procedure to make sure no data is lost.

COUNTRY CODES

Each country has a special code used in domain names. Here are a few examples.

as	Austria
au	Australia
be	Belgium
ca	Canada
ch	Switzerland
de	Germany
es	Spain
fr	France
jp	Japan
nz	New Zealand
uk	United Kingdom
us	United States
za	South Africa

Modem Short for modulator-demodulator. Device that links a computer to a telephone line and enables the user to send faxes and e-mails and gain access to the internet.

Net *see* Internet.

WWW

Network Group of computers linked by cables to each other and to a central server allowing them to share programs and data. The computers may be in separate buildings or separate countries, all linked by telephone. The internet is a planet-wide collection of linked networks.

Nickname False name that you can use to hide your identity when using the internet.

Offline *see* Online.

Online You are online when you are connected to the internet, offline when you close the connection.

org Short for organization. Used in domain names for charities and non-profitmaking organizations.

Password Set of letters and/or numbers that you type into the computer to tell your ISP that it is you and not somebody else using your computer. You also need a password to access information protected by a firewall.

Protocol Set of rules that computers follow when

Ask the person who pays the phone bill before you go online.

BE SAFE

TELL your parents or teacher if you see or read anything on the internet that upsets you

NEVER tell anyone where you live or where you go to school

NEVER give a stranger your phone number or your e-mail address

NEVER give anyone your password

NEVER arrange to meet anyone you do not know already

NEVER meet anyone without asking your parents first

Never give your name or address to strangers.

communicating with each other over the internet.

Safety *see* panel above.

Server Large computer on a network containing programs and data that can be shared with other computers on the same network. You can download files or web pages from servers on the internet.

Service provider *see* ISP.

Upload To send a file to another computer or to a server on the internet.

User name Name adopted by a person using the internet. In

e-mail addresses it appears before the @ sign.

USENET News Part of the internet where electronic discussion groups called newsgroups operate.

Virus Program designed to damage or destroy other programs. You can get software that will search for and delete viruses and clean up your files.

World wide web (WWW) Large part of the internet that consists of hundreds of thousands of documents containing text, pictures, videos and music, and links to other documents.

Get the @ @ message

With a connection to the internet, you can use your computer to send e-mails almost instantly anywhere in the world. Writing to your cousin in Australia can be easier and cheaper than posting a letter to a school friend living round the corner.

@ *see* at.

Address Everyone on the internet has an address. It consists of a user name, telling the world who is receiving the mail, followed by the @ sign, and finally a domain name.

Address book E-mail programs let you keep a file of names and e-mail addresses. The program automatically copies them from e-mails you receive, and you can change them or add new ones.

at The meaning of the sign @ in e-mail addresses.

Attachment Any file from your computer that you add to an e-mail. It may be a text document, picture, sound or video.

bcc Short for blind carbon copy. Type an e-mail address in this box in the header of your message to send a copy of it to a third person without telling the person you are actually writing to what you are doing.

Bouncing mail If you get an address wrong or if an address has changed, your message will bounce back to your mailbox.

You have new mail

OK

44

cc Short for carbon copy. To send the same message to more than one person, fill in this box in the header. You can put in several addresses and everyone you name will receive the message.

E-mail Short for electronic mail. A way of sending messages from your computer to the internet.

E-mail safety *see* panel on page 47.

Emoticons Another word for Smileys. It comes from two words, emotion and icon.

FAQ Short for frequently asked questions. A document that gives beginners useful basic information. Most newsgroups and websites publish FAQs to save new people asking questions that have been answered many times before.

Flaming If you use CAPITAL LETTERS or are rude or offensive in an e-mail or news post, other people may flame you – that is, send you angry e-mails.

Header The top part of an e-mail that tells about the sender, the route the message took across the internet, the subject of the e-mail, and the recipient (the person who received the e-mail).

Inbox In some e-mail programs, the part of your computer's hard disk where the program stores the e-mail that has just arrived.

Junk mail Unwanted e-mail that arrives unexpectedly, usually from people trying to sell you things. It is best to throw it away.

Lurk When you first join a newsgroup or message board, it is a good idea not to send post to it or join in discussions straight away but wait until you get the feel of things. This is called lurking.

Copy addresses exactly. Don't leave gaps.

45

ATCHOO!

Mailbox Place on a computer where an e-mail program stores messages for a particular user.
Mailing list List of the e-mail addresses of people who share an interest and send each other articles. There are hundreds of topics to choose from. If you join a mailing list, you can send messages to lots of people.

Message board Part of a website where you can leave messages, ask questions and make comments.
Netiquette Good manners on the internet, including being brief and being polite. People who break the rules of netiquette run the risk of being flamed.
Newsgroup Internet discussion group dealing with a particular subject in which you can ask questions or make statements about the subject in the form of news posts. Ask permission before you join a newsgroup, and never give out your real name.
Newsreader In order to read posts in a newsgroup or to send posts to it, you need a program called a newsreader.

SHOUTING

Outbox In some e-mail programs, the part of your computer where the program stores the e-mail that is to be sent the next time you go online.

Post Message sent to a newsgroup.

Punctuation marks Full stops, commas, colons, question marks and quotation marks like these – . , : ? " – that help make what you write easier to read. They are also used to make smileys (*see* page 48).

Queue When you finish writing an e-mail but do not want to send it straight away, it goes into a queue with other outgoing e-mails. When you next go online, all the e-mails in the queue are sent off.

Receive When you connect to the internet, you receive any e-mail that is meant for you - that is, your internet service provider automatically moves all the e-mail intended for you onto your computer.

Re:Mail *see* Reply.

Reply Most programs have a way of allowing you to reply to e-mails quickly by clicking the Reply or Re:Mail button.

E-MAIL SAFETY

NEVER give your e-mail address to anyone you do not already know.

NEVER tell anyone where you live or go to school.

NEVER give anyone your phone number.

NEVER arrange to meet anyone you do not already know

NEVER meet anyone without your parents' permission.

Big Grin

Wink

Sad

Send When you connect to the internet, all the e-mail you have in your queue or outbox is automatically uploaded to your internet service provider's computer and from there it goes to its destination. Many e-mail programs have a Send icon or button. When you click on it, your computer automatically goes online and uploads the e-mails you have ready.

Shouting Using CAPITAL LETTERS in an e-mail or news post. It is considered a breach of netiquette.

SMILEYS

Not a Word

:-D	big grin
0:-)	angel
:í-(	boo hoo
:-P	tongue out
:-(	sad
:-{#}	smile in a brace
:-)	happy
:-O	wow
;-)	wink
$-)	greedy
:-x	not a word
:*)	only joking
:-/	what?
:->	knowing grin

Signature Short piece of text added to the end of an e-mail or news post that includes the name by which you want to be known over the internet. It can also include a picture drawn using the letters, numbers and punctuation marks on your keyboard. Signatures longer than five lines may break the rules of Netiquette.

Smileys Pictures made from letters, numbers and punctuation marks that show readers what you are feeling. Also called emoticons.

Spamming Sometimes silly people send copies of stupid or rude messages to lots of people or newsgroups. Internet service providers and newsgroup administrators ban spamming.

Subject Line in the header of an e-mail message or news post that tells the person receiving it what the e-mail is about. E-mail programs provide a box for you to type in the subject.

Subscribe To join a mailing list or newsgroup, or to access an online magazine or newspaper, either for a payment or for free.

Thread When someone sends a post to a newsgroup on a particular subject, others may send posts reacting to it. Newsgroup organizers use software to collect all these related posts together to form a thread.

Save money by saving your messages and sending them together.

Caught in the web

The world wide web is part of the internet. It is like a vast library where the pages in the books do not just have words and pictures, but sounds and movies too. Web pages contain links to other pages, letting you jump straight to what you want to know. But the web is more than a library. You can download files from it, send messages over it, buy and sell things on it, or watch TV or listen to music and radio on it.

Address *see* Web address.

Bookmarks Computer file containing a list of your favourite or most visited websites.

Browser (Web browser) Application that lets you read web pages and find your way around the world wide web. Microsoft Internet Explorer and Netscape Navigator are the best known.

Chatroom Part of the internet where you can have conversations with people who share your interests. You type what you want to say and people online at the same time type their responses. Many websites have chatrooms, but you can also join chat channels. *See* IRC.

Cookie Piece of data passed to your browser from a website you are viewing. It is stored on your computer and sent back to the website each time you visit it. Cookies identify visitors and track access to the site that sent them.

Favorites Name given by Microsoft Internet Explorer to the file of bookmarks it uses. *See also* Bookmarks.

Frame Browsers display web pages in a window on the screen. Some websites present their pages using a window that has been split into separate areas called frames. Early versions of browsers cannot show frames.

Handle Another name for a nickname chosen by an internet user.

Home page Part of a person's or organization's website that a visitor comes to first. It welcomes visitors and provides links to other web pages on the site.

Hotlink Type of connection between two documents causing one document to be automatically updated when the other document is changed. *See also* Link.

HTML Short for hypertext markup language. Set of codes added to a text document and used by a browser to display a web page's words, pictures and so on, in the desired way.

http Short for hypertext transfer protocol. Set of rules that controls the way in which information is passed between servers and client computers over the web. All web addresses start with http:// to tell computers to use this protocol when connecting with websites.

Hyperlink *see* Link.

Hypertext System that connects all web pages so that you can move from one to another by clicking on links or icons.

IRC Short for internet relay chat. Internet channels where you can chat to other people with the same interest. You need a special program to use a chat channel.

Keywords Words placed at the beginning of a web page allowing a search engine to find it and classify it properly.

Spending time on the internet costs money, so always ask first.

Link Connection between one web page and another that a user can click on with a mouse to jump from the page being viewed straight to the connected page. Links are usually in a different colour or are underlined but can also be icons, pictures or 'buttons'. Also called Hyperlink or Hotlink.

Microsoft Internet Explorer Web browser made by Microsoft Corporation.

Netscape Navigator / Communicator Versions of a browser developed by Netscape Communications Corporation.

Proxy server You can choose to view a website either directly through your internet connection or via a proxy server, which looks up the website for you and remembers it if you want to see it again later. Using a proxy server may be quicker than viewing the site directly.

Search engine One of many websites that hold a huge database of other websites sorted into subjects. Type in a subject and the search engine will find suitable websites, displaying the sites it finds. Well-known search engines include Alta Vista, Lycos and Yahoo.

Site *see* Website.

Surfing Moving from one site to another on the web.

URL Short for uniform resource locator. String of letters and symbols telling where you can find a particular site on the net. A URL is usually a web address, but it can also be an e-mail address, FTP site or other resource.

Be as specific as you can when you search.

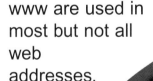

Web address Sequence of words and symbols that enables web browsers to find each site on the web. Each address starts with http:// to tell computers that they are dealing with a file using the hypertext transfer protocol.

Web browser *see* Browser.

Web page Single document downloaded from a website.

Web safety *see* panel.

Website Collection of related web pages held on a server and accessible to internet users.

World wide web Collection of millions of websites containing linked pages that anyone with an internet connection and a browser can look at.

WWW Short for world wide web. The letters www are used in most but not all web addresses.

SAFE SURFING

There are some strange people using the world wide web. They try to trick people into giving them money or they may send someone a destructive computer virus. Follow these sensible guidelines when surfing.

ALWAYS beware of new websites. Some sites that seem harmless contain unpleasant material. If you are worried leave the site immediately.

ALWAYS check any files you download for viruses.

NEVER fill in an online response form without asking your parents first.

NEVER use a chatroom or message board without permission.

NEVER give anyone your real name, your phone number or the name of your school.

ALWAYS tell your parents or your teacher if you see anything that upsets you on the web.

Staying in touch

You do not have to be in any one place to access the internet. With an up-to-date mobile phone, you can read your e-mail, check the football results, or look at a website while you are on the move.

Audio Sound part of a TV broadcast or multimedia data transmission. The picture part is called video.

Bandwidth Amount of data that an internet connection can handle in a given time, measured in bits per second. Different types of data use different amounts of bandwidth. Sound and video use much more than plain text.

bps Short for bits per second. Way of measuring the speed at which digital data is passed along a telephone line or computer connection.

Coaxial cable Cable for transmitting very high frequency currents. It consists of a wire running through, and insulated from, a covering that also allows electricity to flow through it.

Compression (Data compression) Removing unnecessary information from a stream of digital data, making it possible for more information to be transmitted over connections and channels.

Fax Short for Facsimile. Way of transmitting text and pictures over a telephone line. Hard copy placed in a fax machine is read by an electronic scanner. The scanner turns the text or picture into electronic signals that travel over the phone line to a fax machine at the other end, which uses a built-in printer to print out what has been sent.

Fibre-optic cable Cable made from thin strands of glass or plastic. Data is converted into flashes of laser light and sent down the cable to a detector at the other end. The detector turns the on-off laser pulses back into the original data.

Internet phone Way of making cheap telephone calls over the internet using a computer microphone and special software. You and the person you want to talk to must be on the net at the same time.

mbps Short for megabits per second. Way of measuring the speed of a fast computer connection.
See also
bps.

Mobile phone Portable telephone that sends and receives speech, text messages, and other kinds of data as radio waves. Signals travel via tall radio masts controlling transmissions in local areas called cells.

Optical fibre Single strand of clear glass or plastic used in fibre-optic cable. It may be thinner than a human hair. *See* Fibre-optic cable.

Packet Piece of data forming part of a much larger message but which is sent separately. Data may be transmitted by packet-switching, in which a message is broken down into packets. Each packet is sent by the best way possible and the whole message is put back together again at its destination.

It costs more to use a mobile phone than an ordinary phone.

Videoconferencing

Palmtop Small, lightweight computer that can be held in the palm of one hand. Some palmtops may be used as personal digital assistants.

Personal digital assistant Hand-held computer with a keyboard and/or pointing device, business and e-mail software and sometimes the ability to access the internet and the world wide web on the move.

Satellite Small uncrewed spacecraft travelling around the earth. Telecommunications satellites are used for transmitting telephone calls and broadcasts over long distances.

Shorttext *see* panel on page 57.

Telecommunications Branch of industry to do with transmitting speech, text or other information over long distances by various means, including cable, telegraph, telephone, radio, TV, and so on.

Teletext System for transmitting news and information in the form of text and simple graphics using the spare lines of a television picture signal.

Video Moving pictures or the visual part of a TV broadcast or multimedia data transmission. The sound part is known as audio.

Videoconference Meeting between people in different locations in which video cameras and screens connected to telephone lines allow people to see each other as they talk.

Videophone Telephone-like device that transmits and receives pictures as well as sound.

It is **dangerous to use the phone on the move.**

SHORTTEXT

People who send and receive text messages with a mobile phone use a kind of shorthand because they are allowed only 160 characters. Here are a few phrases.

RUF2T	Are you free to talk
FantaC	Fantasy
g%d	Good
IL B L8	I'll be late
NMP	Not my problem
OMG	Oh my goodness
CUL8R	See you later
s%n	Soon
2DA	Today
2moro	Tomorrow
th@	That

Please do not write proper letters or e-mails this way.

WAP Short for wireless application protocol. Set of rules allowing mobile phones and personal digital assistants to gain limited access to the internet over radio or satellite links. WAP phones offer e-mail and text-message services and access to text-based websites.

Wap phone

Going digital

Thanks to digital technology, we can now surf the net through the TV, watch TV on the world wide web, and send e-mails by mobile phone.

Broadcasting Sending out information or programmes to the public by television or radio, using radio waves.

Channel Band of frequencies used for broadcasting radio and television programmes. In the past one channel carried one company's programmes. Digital broadcasting makes it possible to send many different programmes at once over the same frequency band.

Channel hopping Moving quickly from one television channel to another using a remote-control.

Also called channel surfing.

Decoder Device that makes it possible to view a digital or scrambled (deliberately mixed-up) TV broadcast.

Digital broadcasting Form of broadcasting in which the data (a radio or TV show) carried by radio waves is turned into binary digits or bits (0s and 1s). The bits are received by a microprocessor in the TV, radio or set-top box and turned back into the original show.

Frequency Rate at which radio waves carrying a radio or TV broadcast are travelling. Since all radio and light waves travel at the same speed, frequency measures the number of wave crests (tops) that pass by a fixed point in one second. The movement from one crest to the next is called a cycle or hertz.

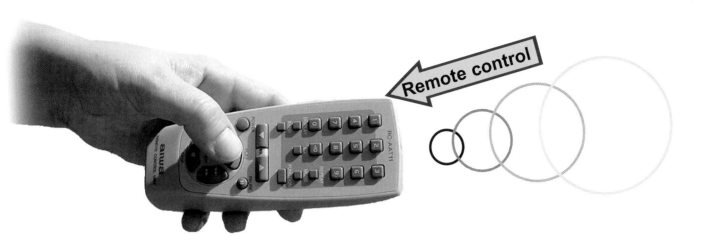

Remote control

Interactive An interactive television show or computer program allows a two-way flow of information between its viewer or user and itself. Online voting and online shopping are examples of interactive television.

Movies on demand System that allows several broadcasts of a movie to take place at roughly the same time, except that successive broadcasts are delayed by a set amount of time, letting individual viewers choose when they want to start watching.

Online voting Pressing one of two or more buttons on a remote-control to make a choice during a TV show.

Pay-per-view Channels or programmes that you receive only if you choose to pay for them.

Set-top box Box containing a microprocessor that connects a TV aerial or satellite dish to a non-digital TV set. It receives digital broadcasts through the aerial or disk and turns them into a form that the TV set can handle.

Wide-screen Form of television broadcast designed for a TV set that shows a wide field of view in relation to its height.

More programmes doesn't mean better programmes.

Buying and selling

Over the internet you can buy anything from a video game to a new car. You can visit your bank or book a holiday without leaving your home. Your computer can keep a track of the way you spend your money, and so can the websites you visit.

ATM Short for automatic teller machine. Computerized machine used by high-street banks to issue cash, supply bank statements and so on, to its customers. You insert a card bearing your bank details into the ATM, type in your PIN and make choices on the screen.

Bar code Pattern of numbers and parallel lines of varying thickness printed on an item for sale. A computer can read the code through a scanner and use the information to keep track of how many items are in stock.

Cart *see* Shopping cart.

Cheque guarantee card Plastic card that carries a person's bank details in a form a computer can read. It also has a special number proving that it is your card. You can use the card to get cash out of an ATM or to prove who you are when writing a cheque. Also called a cheque card or banker's card.

Clicks-and-mortar Describes a company that has high-street shops that you can visit as well as a website on the internet.

Credit card Plastic card that can be used instead of cash or a cheque to make a purchase. The number on the card proves the identity of the owner. Never use anyone else's card.

Decryption Decoding encrypted data or messages. *See also* Encryption.

ISBN 1-84234-056-5

Bar code

9 781842 340547

60

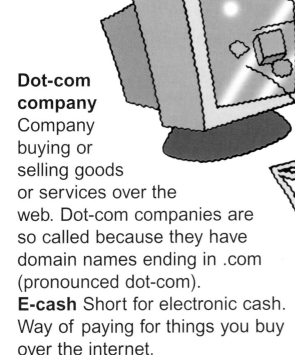

Dot-com company Company buying or selling goods or services over the web. Dot-com companies are so called because they have domain names ending in .com (pronounced dot-com).

E-cash Short for electronic cash. Way of paying for things you buy over the internet.

Encryption Process of hiding data, such as financial details or a credit card number, by turning them into a code that is hard to break. Encrypted data can be passed securely between two computers. *See* Security.

E-tailer Short for electronic retailer. Company that sells things on the web.

Expiry date Date after which a credit card can no longer be used.

Magnetic strip Area on a cheque card or credit card covered with a magnetic layer on which data that can be read by a computer is stored.

Ask before you buy anything and check the price!

9876 1234
6543

PIN numbers

Online banking Process of managing a bank account through the bank's website. Most banks have systems that allow people to pay bills, transfer money from one account to another, and print out statements twenty-four hours a day. Account holders have a password to stop other people interfering with their account.

Online response form Form on a website that you fill in online. You specify items you want to buy and give your name, address and credit card details.

Online shopping Looking for and buying things on the web. Popular online shopping items are books, clothes, computer software and hardware, airline flights and holidays.

Payment Using the internet costs money. You normally have to pay the service provider to connect you and the telephone company for time spent online. If you download certain types of software or games or access the web versions of certain magazines, you may have to pay for them too. Practically everything you buy online has to be paid for by credit card. Always ask permission if you want to buy something on the internet.

PIN Short for personal identification number. Number known only to you that you must type in on a keypad at an ATM or similar

Touchscreen

machine after inserting a card to prove that you are the owner of the card. You can then carry out a chosen action.

Point-of-sale terminal Computer in a shop linked by telephone to a central computer or a credit-card company. It reads bar codes, credit-card details and so on, to process the sale of an item.

Security E-tailers use security measures such as encryption and firewalls to make sure that the financial information they receive from customers stays secret.

Shopping cart Computer file on an e-tailer's website listing items that a buyer wants to purchase, together with quantities and prices. The buyer adds items to the shopping cart by filling in a form or clicking a button. When the buyer is finished, a program running on the website adds up the cost of the items in the shopping cart and bills the buyer's credit card. Also called a shopping trolley.

Smartcard Plastic card with a built-in microprocessor. It is used to make payments, open electronically locked doors and so on.

Statement Printed record of all the money paid into and taken out of a bank or credit-card account.

Touchscreen Computer screen that you touch with your finger to make a choice from a menu. Touchscreens are often used in tills in shops and restaurants.

> Never use somebody else's credit card without asking!

WACKY WEBSITES

Here are some websites for you to visit. Some are useful, others are just fun.

WEB HEALTH

Surfing the net can be fun but it is not safe to do it for too long. You can damage your eyes, strain your muscles and become addicted.

TAKE regular breaks to rest your eyes
TAKE exercise to build your muscles
SPEND time with friends
PLAY outdoor games as well as video games

BROWSERS
Microsoft Internet Explorer: **http://www.microsoft.com/windows/ie/**
Netscape Communicator/Navigator: **http://home.netscape.com/**

SEARCH ENGINES
Ask Jeeves:**http://www.ask.com/**
Lycos: **http://www.lycos.com/**
Yahoo: **http://www.yahoo.com/**
Yahooligans: **http://www.yahooligans.com/**

Have fun!

SOFTWARE
Shareware.com: **http://www.shareware.com/**
Tucows: **http://www.tucows.com/**

FUN AND LEARNING
BBC Online: **http://www.bbc.co.uk/**
Discovery Online: **http://www.discovery.com/online.html**
Disney: **http://www.disney.com/**
Free Internet Encyclopedia: **http://www.encyclopedia.com/**
The Locker Room: **http://members.aol.com/msdaizy/sports/locker.html**
Suite 101: **http://www.suite101.com/links.cfm/230**

Magic Mouse: **http://www.magic-mouse.co.uk**